FOR:_____

$\mathcal{T}$he LORD is my light and my salvation—
   whom shall I fear?
The LORD is the stronghold of my life—
   of whom shall I be afraid?

Psalm 27:1

FROM: _____

Psalms and Proverbs for a Woman of Faith

Copyright 1999 by New Life Clinics

ISBN 0-310-98092-5

WOMEN OF FAITH℠

All Scripture quotations, unless otherwise noted, are taken from the *Holy Bible: New International Version*®, (North American Edition). Copyright 1973, 1978, 1984, by the International Bible Society. Used by permission of Zondervan Publishing House. All rights reserved.

The "NIV" and "New International Version" trademarks are registered in the United States Patent and Trademark Office by International Bible Society.

All rights reserved. No part of this publication may be reproduced, stored in a retrieval system, or transmitted in any form or by any means—electronic, mechanical, photocopy, recording, or any other—except for brief quotations in printed reviews, without the prior permission of the publisher.

Requests for information should be addressed to:

ZondervanPublishingHouse
Grand Rapids, Michigan 49530
http://www.zondervan.com

Director of Gift Products: Gwen Ellis
Project Editor: Pat Matuszak

Printed in China

00 01 02 /HK/ 4 3 2

PSALMS AND PROVERBS FOR A WOMAN OF FAITH

Zondervan*Gifts*

We have a gift for inspiration™

PSALMS AND PROVERBS FOR A WOMAN OF FAITH

ON

Praising God
Prayer
The Gift of Forgiveness
God's Care for Us
Promises of Protection
God's Healing Mercy
Living with Integrity
Trusting God
The Treasure of Wisdom
The Love of God, Family, and Friends

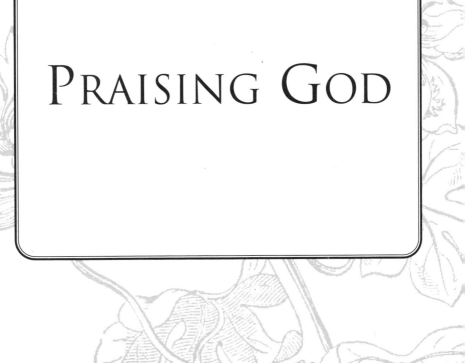

PRAISING GOD

The Lord lives! Praise be to my Rock!
  Exalted be God my Savior!
Therefore I will praise you among the nations, O
    Lord;
  I will sing praises to your name.

Psalm 18:46, 49

❧

I will give thanks to the Lord because of his
    righteousness
  and will sing praise to the name of the Lord
    Most High.

Psalm 7:17

❧

In the congregation I will praise you.

Psalm 22:22

From the lips of children and infants
you have ordained praise.

Psalm 8:2

❧

I will praise you, O LORD, with all my heart;
I will tell of all your wonders.
I will be glad and rejoice in you;
I will sing praise to your name, O Most High.

Psalm 9:1–2

❧

Praise awaits you, O God, in Zion;
to you our vows will be fulfilled.

Psalm 65:1

From you comes the theme of my praise in the great
    assembly;
  before those who fear you will I fulfill my vows.
The poor will eat and be satisfied;
  they who seek the Lord will praise him—
  may your hearts live forever!
All the ends of the earth
  will remember and turn to the Lord,
and all the families of the nations
  will bow down before him,
for dominion belongs to the Lord
  and he rules over the nations.
All the rich of the earth will feast and worship;
  all who go down to the dust will kneel before him—
  those who cannot keep themselves alive.
Posterity will serve him;
  future generations will be told about the Lord.
They will proclaim his righteousness
  to a people yet unborn.

Psalm 22:25–31

*Y*ou are enthroned as the Holy One;
    you are the praise of Israel
In you our fathers put their trust;
    they trusted and you delivered them.

Psalm 22:3–4

❧

I wash my hands in innocence,
    and go about your altar, O LORD,
proclaiming aloud your praise
    and telling of all your wonderful deeds.

Psalm 26:6–7

Sing to the LORD, you saints of his;
   praise his holy name.

Psalm 30:4

❧

Sing joyfully to the LORD, you righteous;
   it is fitting for the upright to praise him.
Praise the LORD with the harp;
   make music to him on the ten-stringed lyre.
Sing to him a new song;
   play skillfully, and shout for joy.
For the word of the LORD is right and true;
   he is faithful in all he does.

Psalm 33:1–4

Praise be to the LORD,
   for he showed his wonderful love to me
   when I was in a besieged city.

Psalm 31:21

❧

I will extol the LORD at all times;
   his praise will always be on my lips.
My soul will boast in the LORD;
   let the afflicted hear and rejoice.
Glorify the LORD with me;
   let us exalt his name together.
I sought the LORD, and he answered me;
   he delivered me from all my fears.
Those who look to him are radiant.

Psalm 34:1–5

$\mathcal{H}$e put a new song in my mouth,
    a hymn of praise to our God.
Many will see and fear
    and put their trust in the LORD.
Blessed is the man
    who makes the LORD his trust,
who does not look to the proud,
    to those who turn aside to false gods.
Many, O LORD my God,
    are the wonders you have done.
The things you planned for us
    no one can recount to you;
were I to speak and tell of them
    they would be too many to declare.

Psalm 40:3–5

Within your temple, O God,
  we meditate on your unfailing love.
Like your name, O God,
  your praise reaches to the ends of the earth;
  your right hand is filled with righteousness.

Psalm 48:9–10

❧

Then will I go to the altar of God,
  to God, my joy and my delight.
I will praise you with the harp
  O God, my God.
Why are you downcast, O my soul?
  Why so disturbed within me?
Put your hope in God,
  for I will yet praise him,
  my Savior and my God.

Psalm 43:4–5

*W*hy are you downcast, O my soul?
    Why so disturbed within me?
Put your hope in God,
    for I will yet praise him
    my Savior and my God.
My soul is downcast within me;
    therefore I will remember you.

Psalm 42:5–6

❧

I will sacrifice a freewill offering to you;
    I will praise your name, O LORD,
    for it is good.
For he has delivered me from all my troubles,
    and my eyes have looked in triumph on my foes.

Psalm 54:6–7

PRAYER

If you call out for insight
  and cry aloud for understanding,
and if you look for it as for silver
  and search for it as for hidden treasure,
then you will understand the fear of the LORD
  and find the knowledge of God.

Proverbs 2:3–5

⚜

My soul waits for the Lord
  more than watchmen wait for the morning,
  more than watchmen wait for the morning.

Psalm 130:6

Deep calls to deep
in the roar of your waterfalls;
all your waves and breakers
have swept over me.
By day the LORD directs his love,
at night his song is with me—
a prayer to the God of my life.

Psalm 42:7–8

❧

Give ear to my words, O LORD,
consider my sighing.
Listen to my cry for help,
my King and my God,
for to you I pray.
In the morning, O LORD, you hear my voice;
in the morning I lay my requests before you
and wait in expectation.

Psalm 5:1–3

I pray to you, O Lord,
    in the time of your favor;
in your great love, O God,
    answer me with your sure salvation.

Psalm 69:13

❧

Answer me when I call to you,
    O my righteous God.
Give me relief from my distress;
    be merciful to me and hear my prayer.

Psalm 4:1

*H*ear, O LORD, my righteous plea;
   listen to my cry.
Give ear to my prayer—
   it does not rise from deceitful lips. . . .
My steps have held to your paths;
   my feet have not slipped.
I call on you, O God, for you will answer me;
   give ear to me and hear my prayer.
Show the wonder of your great love,
   you who save by your right hand
   those who take refuge in you from their foes.
Keep me as the apple of your eye;
   hide me in the shadow of your wings.

Psalm 17:1, 5–8

Hear my prayer, O LORD,
    listen to my cry for help;
    be not deaf to my weeping.

Psalm 39:12

❧

Save me, O God, by your name;
    vindicate me by your might.
Hear my prayer, O God;
    listen to the words of my mouth....
Surely God is my help;
    the Lord is the one who sustains me.

Psalm 54:1–2, 4

❧

Two things I ask of you, O LORD...
Keep falsehood and lies far from me;
    give me neither poverty nor riches,
    but give me only my daily bread.

Proverbs 30:7–8

Hear my cry, O God;
    listen to my prayer.
From the ends of the earth I call to you,
    I call as my heart grows faint;
    lead me to the rock that is higher than I.

Psalm 61:1–2

❧

If I had cherished sin in my heart,
    the Lord would not have listened;
but God has surely listened
    and heard my voice in prayer.
Praise be to God,
    who has not rejected my prayer
    or withheld his love from me!

Psalm 66:18–20

Hear my prayer, O LORD God Almighty;
   listen to me, O God of Jacob.
Look upon our shield, O God;
   look with favor on your anointed one.
Better is one day in your courts
   than a thousand elsewhere;
I would rather be a doorkeeper in the house of my God
   than dwell in the tents of the wicked.

Psalm 84:8–10

❧

The lips of the wise spread knowledge;
   not so the hearts of fools.
The LORD detests the sacrifice of the wicked,
   but the prayer of the upright pleases him.

Proverbs 15:7–8

Have mercy on me, O Lord,
   for I call to you all day long.
Bring joy to your servant,
   for to you, O Lord,
   I lift up my soul.
You are forgiving and good, O Lord,
   abounding in love to all who call to you.
Hear my prayer, O LORD;
   listen to my cry for mercy.
In the day of my trouble I will call to you,
   for you will answer me.

Psalm 86:3–7

❧

Let everyone who is godly pray to you
   while you may be found.

Psalm 32:6

$\mathcal{O}$ LORD, the God who saves me,
   day and night I cry out before you.
May my prayer come before you;
   turn your ear to my cry....
I cry to you for help, O LORD;
   in the morning my prayer comes before you.

Psalm 88:1–2, 13

❧

$\mathcal{H}$ear my prayer, O LORD;
   let my cry for help come to you.
Do not hide your face from me
   when I am in distress.
Turn your ear to me;
   when I call, answer me quickly.

Psalm 102:1–2

O LORD, I call to you; come quickly to me.
   Hear my voice when I call to you.
May my prayer be set before you like incense;
   may the lifting up of my hands be like the
      evening sacrifice.

Psalm 141:1–2

❧

O LORD, hear my prayer,
   listen to my cry for mercy;
in your faithfulness and righteousness
   come to my relief.

Psalm 143:1

❧

*T*he heart of the righteous weighs its answers, . . .
The LORD is far from the wicked
   but he hears the prayer of the righteous.

Proverbs 15:28–29

*H*e will respond to the prayer of the destitute;
   he will not despise their plea.

Psalm 102:17

❧

*L*isten to my prayer, O God,
   do not ignore my plea;
hear me and answer me.

Psalm 55:1–2

❧

I lift up my eyes to you,
   to you whose throne is in heaven.

Psalm 123:1

THE GIFT OF
FORGIVENESS

Forgive my hidden faults.
Keep your servant also from willful sins;
    may they not rule over me.
Then will I be blameless,
    innocent of great transgression.
May the words of my mouth and the meditation of
        my heart
    be pleasing in your sight,
O LORD, my Rock and my Redeemer.

Psalm 19:12–14

☙

Even a child is known by his actions,
    by whether his conduct is pure and right.
Ears that hear and eyes that see—
    the LORD has made them both.

Proverbs 20:11–12

*B*lessed is he
    whose transgressions are forgiven,
    whose sins are covered...
    whose sin the LORD does not count against him
    and in whose spirit is no deceit.
When I kept silent,
    my bones wasted away
    through my groaning all day long....
Then I acknowledged my sin to you
    and did not cover up my iniquity.
I said, "I will confess
    my transgressions to the LORD"—
and you forgave
    the guilt of my sin.
Therefore let everyone who is godly pray to you
    while you may be found;
surely when the mighty waters rise,
    they will not reach him.
You are my hiding place;
    you will protect me from trouble
    and surround me with songs of deliverance

Psalm 32:1–3, 5–7

O Lord, hear my voice.
Let your ears be attentive
  to my cry for mercy.
If you, O LORD, kept a record of sins,
  O Lord, who could stand?
But with you there is forgiveness;
  therefore you are feared.
I wait for the LORD, my soul waits,
  and in his word I put my hope.

Psalm 130:2–5

❧

*A*n evil man is snared by his own sin,
  but a righteous one can sing and be glad.

Proverbs 29:6

All the ways of the LORD are loving and faithful
  for those who keep the demands of his
    covenant.
For the sake of your name, O LORD,
  forgive my iniquity, though it is great....
My eyes are ever on the LORD,
  for only he will release my feet from the snare.
Turn to me and be gracious to me,
  for I am lonely and afflicted.
The troubles of my heart have multiplied;
  free me from my anguish.
Look upon my affliction and my distress
  and take away all my sins.

Psalm 25:10–11, 15–18

Through love and faithfulness sin is atoned for;
  through the fear of the LORD a man avoids evil.

Proverbs 16:6

❧

He who conceals his sins does not prosper,
  but whoever confesses and renounces them finds
    mercy.

Proverbs 28:13

❧

The Lord provided redemption for his people;
  he ordained his covenant forever—
  holy and awesome is his name.

Psalm 111:9

Restore us, O God;
   make your face shine upon us,
   that we may be saved.

Psalm 80:3

❧

I, by your great mercy,
   will come into your house;
in reverence will I bow down
   toward your holy temple.
Lead me, O LORD, in your righteousness
   because of my enemies—
   make straight your way before me.

Psalm 5:7–8

To you I call, O LORD my Rock;
    do not turn a deaf ear to me.
For if you remain silent,
    I will be like those who have gone down
        to the pit.
Hear my cry for mercy
    as I call to you for help,
as I lift up my hands
    toward your Most Holy Place.

Psalm 28:1–2

Show me your ways, O LORD,
    teach me your paths;
guide me in your truth and teach me,
    for you are God my Savior,
    and my hope is in you all day long.
Remember, O LORD, your great mercy and love,
    for they are from of old.
Remember not the sins of my youth
    and my rebellious ways;
according to your love remember me,
    for you are good, O LORD.
Good and upright is the LORD;
    therefore he instructs sinners in his ways.
He guides the humble in what is right
    and teaches them his way.

Psalm 25:4–9

Praise be to the LORD,
　　for he has heard my cry for mercy.
The LORD is my strength and my shield;
　　my heart trusts in him, and I am helped.
My heart leaps for joy
　　and I will give thanks to him in song.
The LORD is the strength of his people,
　　a fortress of salvation for his anointed one.
Save your people and bless your inheritance;
　　be their shepherd and carry them forever.

Psalm 28:6–9

$\mathcal{O}$ Lord, open my lips,
  and my mouth will declare your praise.
You do not delight in sacrifice, or I would bring it;
  you do not take pleasure in burnt offerings.
The sacrifices of God are a broken spirit;
  a broken and contrite heart,
  O God, you will not despise.

Psalm 51:15–17

Have mercy on me, O God,
    according to your unfailing love;
according to your great compassion
    blot out my transgressions.
Wash away all my iniquity
    and cleanse me from my sin.
For I know my transgressions,
    and my sin is always before me.
Against you, you only, have I sinned
    and done what is evil in your sight,
so that you are proved right when you speak
    and justified when you judge.

Psalm 51:1–4

❧

God mocks proud mockers
    but gives grace to the humble.

Proverbs 3:34

Cleanse me with hyssop, and I will be clean;
    wash me, and I will be whiter than snow.
Let me hear joy and gladness;
    let the bones you have crushed rejoice.
Hide your face from my sins
    and blot out all my iniquity.
Create in me a pure heart, O God,
    and renew a steadfast spirit within me.
Do not cast me from your presence
    or take your Holy Spirit from me.
Restore to me the joy of your salvation
    and grant me a willing spirit, to sustain me.

Psalm 51:7–12

$\mathcal{O}$ you who hear prayer,
　　to you all men will come.
When we were overwhelmed by sins,
　　you forgave our transgressions.

Psalm 65:2–3

❧

$\mathcal{D}$o not hold against us the sins of the fathers;
　　may your mercy come quickly to meet us,
　　for we are in desperate need.
Help us, O God our Savior,
　　for the glory of your name;
deliver us and forgive our sins
　　for your name's sake.

Psalm 79:8–9

GOD'S CARE
FOR US

The LORD is the great God,
  the great King above all gods.
In his hand are the depths of the earth,
  and the mountain peaks belong to him.
The sea is his, for he made it,
  and his hands formed the dry land.
Come, let us bow down in worship,
  let us kneel before the LORD our Maker;
for he is our God
  and we are the people of his pasture,
  the flock under his care.

Psalm 95:3–7

❧

The LORD does not let the righteous go hungry....
The blessing of the LORD brings wealth,
  and he adds no trouble to it.

Proverbs 10:3, 22

*W*hoever gives heed to instruction prospers,
   and blessed is he who trusts in the LORD.

Proverbs 16:20

❧

O LORD, our Lord,
   how majestic is your name in all the earth!
You have set your glory
   above the heavens.
From the lips of children and infants
   you have ordained praise
because of your enemies,
   to silence the foe and the avenger.
When I consider your heavens,
   the work of your fingers,
 the moon and the stars,
   which you have set in place,
what is man that you are mindful of him,
   the son of man that you care for him?

Psalm 8:1–4

*B*lessed are those you choose
    and bring near to live in your courts!
We are filled with the good things of your house,
    of your holy temple.
You answer us with awesome deeds of righteousness,
    O God our Savior,
the hope of all the ends of the earth
    and of the farthest seas,
who formed the mountains by your power,
    having armed yourself with strength,
who stilled the roaring of the seas,
    the roaring of their waves,
    and the turmoil of the nations.
Those living far away fear your wonders;
    where morning dawns and evening fades
    you call forth songs of joy.

Psalm 65:4–8

You made him a little lower than the heavenly
        beings
    and crowned him with glory and honor.
You made him ruler over the works of your hands;
    you put everything under his feet:
all flocks and herds,
    and the beasts of the field,
the birds of the air,
    and the fish of the sea,
    all that swim the paths of the seas.
O LORD, our Lord,
    how majestic is your name in all the earth!

Psalm 8:5–9

You care for the land and water it;
    you enrich it abundantly.
The streams of God are filled with water
    to provide the people with grain,
    for so you have ordained it.
You drench its furrows
    and level its ridges;
you soften it with showers
    and bless its crops.
You crown the year with your bounty,
    and your carts overflow with abundance.
The grasslands of the desert overflow;
    the hills are clothed with gladness.
The meadows are covered with flocks
    and the valleys are mantled with grain;
    they shout for joy and sing.

Psalm 65:9–13

The LORD gives strength to his people;
  the LORD blesses his people with peace.

Psalm 29:11

❧

Turn from evil and do good;
  then you will dwell in the land forever.
For the LORD loves the just
  and will not forsake his faithful ones.
They will be protected forever,
  but the offspring of the wicked will be cut off;
the righteous will inherit the land
  and dwell in it forever.

Psalm 37:27–29

Sing to the LORD with thanksgiving;
  make music to our God on the harp.
He covers the sky with clouds;
  he supplies the earth with rain
  and makes grass grow on the hills.
He provides food for the cattle
  and for the young ravens when they call.
His pleasure is not in the strength of the horse,
  nor his delight in the legs of a man;
the LORD delights in those who fear him,
  who put their hope in his unfailing love.
Extol the LORD, O Jerusalem;
  praise your God, O Zion,
for he strengthens the bars of your gates
  and blesses your people within you.
He grants peace to your borders
  and satisfies you with the finest of wheat.

Psalm 147:7–14

$\mathcal{G}$reat are the works of the LORD;
   they are pondered by all who delight in them.
Glorious and majestic are his deeds,
   and his righteousness endures forever.
He has caused his wonders to be remembered;
   the LORD is gracious and compassionate.
He provides food for those who fear him;
   he remembers his covenant forever.
He has shown his people the power of his works,
   giving them the lands of other nations.
The works of his hands are faithful and just;
   all his precepts are trustworthy.
They are steadfast for ever and ever,
   done in faithfulness and uprightness.

Psalm 111:2–8

I lie down and sleep;
  I wake again, because the LORD sustains me.
> *Psalm 3:5*

❧

*Y*ou have upheld my right and my cause;
  you have sat on your throne, judging righteously.
> *Psalm 9:4*

❧

*T*he LORD watches over the way of the righteous.
> *Psalm 1:6*

❧

*Y*ou are a shield around me, O LORD;
  you bestow glory on me and lift up my head.
> *Psalm 3:3*

PROMISES OF
PROTECTION

May the LORD answer you when you are in
     distress;
    may the name of the God of Jacob protect you.
May he send you help from the sanctuary
    and grant you support from Zion.
May he remember all your sacrifices
    and accept your burnt offerings.
May he give you the desire of your heart
    and make all your plans succeed.

Psalm 20:1–4

My eyes are ever on the LORD,
    for only he will release my feet from the snare.
Turn to me and be gracious to me,
    for I am lonely and afflicted.
Look upon my affliction and my distress
    and take away all my sins.
Guard my life and rescue me;
    let me not be put to shame,
    for I take refuge in you.
May integrity and uprightness protect me,
    because my hope is in you.

Psalm 25:15–16, 18, 20–21

*Y*ou are my hiding place;
   you will protect me from trouble
   and surround me with songs of deliverance.
I will instruct you and teach you in the way you
         should go;
   I will counsel you and watch over you.

Psalm 32:7–8

❧

O LORD, you will keep us safe
   and protect us.

Psalm 12:7

I do not hide your righteousness in my heart;
    I speak of your faithfulness and salvation.
I do not conceal your love and your truth
    from the great assembly.
Do not withhold your mercy from me, O LORD;
    may your love and your truth always protect me.
For troubles without number surround me;
    my sins have overtaken me, and I cannot see.
They are more than the hairs of my head,
    and my heart fails within me.
Be pleased, O LORD, to save me;
    O LORD, come quickly to help me.

Psalm 40:10–13

"Because of the oppression of the weak
  and the groaning of the needy,
I will now arise," says the LORD.
  "I will protect them from those who malign them."

Psalm 12:5

❧

"Because he loves me," says the LORD,
  "I will rescue him;
  I will protect him, for he acknowledges my name."

Psalm 91:14

❧

O LORD my God, I take refuge in you;
  save and deliver me from all who pursue me.

Psalm 7:1

Let the righteous rejoice in the LORD
  and take refuge in him;
  let all the upright in heart praise him!

Psalm 64:10

❧

He holds victory in store for the upright,
  he is a shield to those whose walk is blameless,
for he guards the course of the just
  and protects the way of his faithful ones.
Then you will understand what is right and just
  and fair—every good path.
For wisdom will enter your heart,
  and knowledge will be pleasant to your soul.
Discretion will protect you,
  and understanding will guard you.
Wisdom will save you from the ways of wicked men.

Proverbs 2:7–12

May your salvation, O God, protect me.
I will praise God's name in song
    and glorify him with thanksgiving.
This will please the LORD more than an ox,
    more than a bull with its horns and hoofs.
The poor will see and be glad—
    you who seek God, may your hearts live!
The LORD hears the needy
    and does not despise his captive people.

Psalm 69:29–33

*Y*our righteousness is like the mighty mountains,
  your justice like the great deep.
O LORD, you preserve both man and beast.
  How priceless is your unfailing love!
Both high and low among men
  find refuge in the shadow of your wings.
They feast on the abundance of your house;
  you give them drink from your river of delights.
For with you is the fountain of life
  in your light we see light.
Continue your love to those who know you,
  your righteousness to the upright in heart.

Psalm 36:6–10

He will defend the afflicted among the people
and save the children of the needy;
he will crush the oppressor.
He will endure as long as the sun,
as long as the moon, through all generations.
He will be like rain falling on a mown field,
like showers watering the earth.
In his days the righteous will flourish;
prosperity will abound till the moon is no more....
All kings will bow down to him
and all nations will serve him.
For he will deliver the needy who cry out,
the afflicted who have no one to help.
He will take pity on the weak and the needy
and save the needy from death.
He will rescue them from oppression and violence,
for precious is their blood in his sight.

Psalm 72:4–7, 11–14

GOD'S
HEALING
MERCY

Be merciful to me, LORD, for I am faint;
O LORD, heal me, for my bones are in agony.
My soul is in anguish.
Turn, O LORD, and deliver me;
save me because of your unfailing love.

Psalm 6:2–4

❧

Pleasant words are a honeycomb,
sweet to the soul and healing to the bones.

Proverbs 16:24

$\mathscr{B}$lessed is he who has regard for the weak;
    the LORD delivers him in times of trouble.
The LORD will protect him and preserve his life;
    he will bless him in the land
    and not surrender him to the desire of his foes.
The LORD will sustain him on his sickbed
    and restore him from his bed of illness.
I said, "O LORD, have mercy on me;
    heal me, for I have sinned against you."

Psalm 41:1–4

❦

$\mathscr{T}$he tongue of the wise brings healing.
    Truthful lips endure forever.

Proverbs 12:18–19

Trust in the LORD with all your heart
    and lean not on your own understanding;
in all your ways acknowledge him,
    and he will make your paths straight.
Do not be wise in your own eyes;
    fear the LORD and shun evil.
This will bring health to your body
    and nourishment to your bones.
Honor the LORD with your wealth,
    with the firstfruits of all your crops;
then your barns will be filled to overflowing,
    and your vats will brim over with new wine.

Proverbs 3:5–10

The path of the righteous is like the first gleam
  of dawn,
 shining ever brighter till the full light of day.
But the way of the wicked is like deep darkness;
 they do not know what makes them stumble.
Pay attention to what I say
 listen closely to my words.
Do not let them out of your sight,
 keep them within your heart;
for they are life to those who find them…
Above all else, guard your heart,
 for it is the wellspring of life.

Proverbs 4:18–23

A cheerful look brings joy to the heart,
    and good news gives health to the bones.
He who listens to a life-giving rebuke
    will be at home among the wise.

Proverbs 15:30–31

❧

*L*et all who take refuge in you be glad;
    let them ever sing for joy.
Spread your protection over them,
    that those who love your name may rejoice in you.
For surely, O Lord, you bless the righteous;
    you surround them with your favor as with a
        shield.

Psalm 5:11–12

The LORD has heard my weeping.
The LORD has heard my cry for mercy;
　　the LORD accepts my prayer.

Psalm 6:8–9

❧

Remember, O LORD, your great mercy and love,
　　for they are from of old.
Remember not the sins of my youth
　　and my rebellious ways;
according to your love remember me,
　　for you are good, O LORD.

Psalm 25:6–7

Praise be to the LORD, for he has heard my cry for
        mercy.
The LORD is my strength and my shield;
    my heart trusts in him, and I am helped.
My heart leaps for joy
    and I will give thanks to him in song.

Psalm 28:6–7

❧

I will exalt you, O LORD,
    for you lifted me out of the depths.
    and did not let my enemies gloat over me.
O LORD my God, I called to you for help
    and you healed me.
O LORD, you brought me up from the grave;
    you spared me from going down into the pit.

Psalm 30:1–3

O LORD, be my help.
You turned my wailing into dancing;
   you removed my sackcloth and clothed me
      with joy
that my heart may sing to you and not be silent.
   O LORD my God, I will give you thanks forever.

Psalm 30:10–12

❧

*I*n my alarm I said,
   "I am cut off from your sight!"
Yet you heard my cry for mercy
   when I called to you for help.
Love the LORD, all his saints!
   The LORD preserves the faithful,
but the proud he pays back in full.
   Be strong and take heart,
all you who hope in the LORD.

Psalm 31:22–24

In you my soul takes refuge.
I will take refuge in the shadow of your wings
    until the disaster has passed.
I cry out to God Most High,
    to God, who fulfills his purpose for me.

Psalm 57:1–2

༜

You, O Lord, are a compassionate and gracious God,
    slow to anger, abounding in love and faithfulness.
Turn to me and have mercy on me;
    grant your strength to your servant.

Psalm 86:15–16

I was overcome by trouble and sorrow.
Then I called on the name of the LORD:
    "O LORD, save me!"
The LORD is gracious and righteous;
    our God is full of compassion.
The LORD protects the simplehearted;
    when I was in great need, he saved me.
Be at rest once more, O my soul,
    for the LORD has been good to you.
For you, O LORD, have delivered my soul from death,
    my eyes from tears,
    my feet from stumbling,
that I may walk before the LORD
    in the land of the living.

Psalm 116:3–9

$\mathcal{O}$ LORD, have mercy on me;
    raise me up.

Psalm 41:10

❧

$\mathcal{A}$ nswer me, O LORD, out of the goodness of your
        love;
    in your great mercy turn to me.

Psalm 69:16

❧

$\mathcal{I}$ love the LORD, for he heard my voice;
    he heard my cry for mercy.
Because he turned his ear to me,
    I will call on him as long as I live.

Psalm 116:1–2

LIVING WITH INTEGRITY

*B*lessed are they whose ways are blameless,
    who walk according to the law of the Lord.
Blessed are they who keep his statutes
    and seek him with all their heart.

Psalm 119:1-2

∾

*W*hoever of you loves life
    and desires to see many good days,
keep your tongue from evil
    and your lips from speaking lies.
Turn from evil and do good;
    seek peace and pursue it.
The eyes of the Lord are on the righteous
    and his ears are attentive to their cry.

Psalm 34:12–15

$\mathscr{D}$o not withhold good from those who deserve it,
    when it is in your power to act.
Do not say to your neighbor,
    "Come back later; I'll give it tomorrow"—
    when you now have it with you.
Do not plot harm against your neighbor,
    who lives trustfully near you.
Do not accuse a man for no reason—
    when he has done you no harm.

Proverbs 3:27–30

❧

$\mathscr{A}$ good name is more desirable than great riches,
    to be esteemed is better than silver or gold.

Proverbs 22:1

O righteous God,
　　who searches minds and hearts,
bring to an end the violence of the wicked
　　and make the righteous secure.
My shield is God Most High,
　　who saves the upright in heart.

Psalm 7:9–10

❧

G uard my life and rescue me;
　　let me not be put to shame,
　　for I take refuge in you.
May integrity and uprightness protect me,
　　because my hope is in you.

Psalm 25:20–21

In my integrity you uphold me
    and set me in your presence forever.
Praise be to the LORD, the God of Israel,
    from everlasting to everlasting.
    Amen and Amen.

Psalm 41:12–13

❧

The memory of the righteous will be a blessing, . . .
The wise in heart accept commands, . . .
The man of integrity walks securely,
    but he who takes crooked paths will be found out.

Proverbs 10:7–9

The LORD abhors dishonest scales,
  but accurate weights are his delight.
When pride comes, then comes disgrace,
  but with humility comes wisdom.
The integrity of the upright guides them,
  but the unfaithful are destroyed by their duplicity.
Wealth is worthless in the day of wrath,
  but righteousness delivers from death.
The righteousness of the blameless makes a straight way
      for them,
    but the wicked are brought down by their own
      wickedness.
The righteousness of the upright delivers them,
  but the unfaithful are trapped by evil desires.

Proverbs 11:1–6

There is deceit in the hearts of those who plot evil,
   but joy for those who promote peace.

Proverbs 12:20

✌

The highway of the upright avoids evil;
   he who guards his way guards his life.
Pride goes before destruction,
   a haughty spirit before a fall.
Better to be lowly in spirit and among the oppressed
   than to share plunder with the proud.

Proverbs 16:17–19

An honest answer
is like a kiss on the lips.

Proverbs 24:26

❧

The LORD reigns forever;
he has established his throne for judgment.
He will judge the world in righteousness;
he will govern the peoples with justice.
The LORD is a refuge for the oppressed,
a stronghold in times of trouble.
Those who know your name will trust in you,
for you, LORD, have never forsaken those who seek
you.
Sing praises to the LORD, enthroned in Zion;
proclaim among the nations what he has done.

Psalm 9:7–11

A man finds joy in giving an apt reply—
  and how good is a timely word!
The path of life leads upward for the wise
  to keep him from going down to the grave.

Proverbs 15:23–24

❧

*F*or the word of the LORD is right and true;
  he is faithful in all he does.
The LORD loves righteousness and justice
  the earth is full of his unfailing love....
Let all the earth fear the LORD;
  let all the people of the world revere him.

Psalm 33:4–5, 8

Commit your way to the LORD;
    trust in him and he will do this:
He will make your righteousness shine like the dawn,
    the justice of your cause like the noonday sun.
Be still before the LORD and wait patiently for him;
    do not fret when men succeed in their ways,
    when they carry out their wicked schemes.
Refrain from anger and turn from wrath;
    do not fret—it leads only to evil.
For evil men will be cut off,
    but those who hope in the LORD will inherit the land.

Psalm 37:5–9

$\mathcal{R}$ighteousness and justice are the foundation of
        your throne;
    love and faithfulness go before you.
Blessed are those who have learned to acclaim you,
    who walk in the light of your presence, O LORD.
They rejoice in your name all day long
    they exult in your righteousness.
For you are their glory and strength,
    and by your favor you exalt our horn.
Indeed, our shield belongs to the LORD,
    our king to the Holy One of Israel.

Psalm 89:14–18

I will sing of your love and justice;
    to you, O LORD, I will sing praise.
I will be careful to lead a blameless life—
    when will you come to me?
I will walk in my house
    with blameless heart.
My eyes will be on the faithful in the land,
    that they may dwell with me;
he whose walk is blameless
    will minister to me.
No one who practices deceit
    will dwell in my house;
no one who speaks falsely
    will stand in my presence.

Psalm 101:1–2, 6–7

Who can proclaim the mighty acts of the LORD
   or fully declare his praise?
Blessed are they who maintain justice,
   who constantly do what is right.

Psalm 106:2–3

❧

Even in darkness light dawns for the upright,
   for the gracious and compassionate and
      righteous man.
Good will come to him who is generous and lends
      freely,
   who conducts his affairs with justice.

Psalm 112:4–5

❧

It is not good to be partial to the wicked
   or to deprive the innocent of justice.

Proverbs 18:5

Those who forsake the law praise the wicked,
  but those who keep the law resist them.
Evil men do not understand justice,
  but those who seek the LORD understand it fully.
Better a poor man whose walk is blameless
  than a rich man whose ways are perverse.

Proverbs 28:4–6

❧

The righteous care about justice for the poor,
  but the wicked have no such concern.

Proverbs 29:7

❧

If a man shuts his ears to the cry of the poor,
  he too will cry out and not be answered.

Proverbs 21:13

For the LORD is righteous,
    he loves justice;
    upright men will see his face.

Psalm 11:7

❧

LORD, who may dwell in your sanctuary?
    Who may live on your holy hill?
He whose walk is blameless
    and who does what is righteous,
who speaks the truth from his heart
    and has no slander on his tongue,
who does his neighbor no wrong
    and casts no slur on his fellowman, . . .
who keeps his oath
    even when it hurts,
who lends his money without usury
    and does not accept a bribe against the innocent.
He who does these things
    will never be shaken.

Psalm 15:1–5

$\mathcal{D}$o not be wise in your own eyes;
  fear the LORD and shun evil.
This will bring health to your body
  and nourishment to your bones.

Proverbs 3:7–8

❧

$\mathcal{A}$ lying tongue hates those it hurts,
  and a flattering mouth works ruin.

Proverbs 26:28

❧

$\mathcal{D}$o not boast about tomorrow,
  for you do not know what a day may bring forth.
Let another praise you, and not your own mouth;
  someone else, and not your own lips.

Proverbs 27:1–2

TRUSTING GOD

Trust in the LORD with all your heart
 and lean not on your own understanding;
in all your ways acknowledge him,
 and he will make your paths straight.

Proverbs 3:5–6

Know that the LORD has set apart the godly for
    himself;
  the LORD will hear when I call to him.
In your anger do not sin;
  when you are on your beds,
  search your hearts and be silent.
Offer right sacrifices and
  trust in the LORD.
Many are asking, "Who can show us any good?"
  Let the light of your face shine upon us, O LORD.
You have filled my heart with greater joy
  than when their grain and new wine abound.
I will lie down and sleep in peace,
  for you alone, O LORD,
  make me dwell in safety.

Psalm 4:3–8

$\mathcal{I}$ trust in your unfailing love;
　　my heart rejoices in your salvation.
I will sing to the Lord,
　　for he has been good to me.

Psalm 13:5–6

❧

$\mathcal{N}$ow I know that the Lord saves his anointed;
　　he answers him from his holy heaven
　　with the saving power of his right hand.
Some trust in chariots and some in horses,
　　but we trust in the name of the Lord our God.
They are brought to their knees and fall,
　　but we rise up and stand firm.

Psalm 20:6–8

In you our fathers put their trust;
   they trusted and you delivered them.
They cried to you and were saved;
   in you they trusted and were not disappointed....
You brought me out of the womb;
   you made me trust in you
   even at my mother's breast.
From birth I was cast upon you;
   from my mother's womb you have been my
      God.
Do not be far from me.

Psalm 22:4–5, 9–11

To you, O Lord, I lift up my soul;
    in you I trust, O my God.
Do not let me be put to shame,
    nor let my enemies triumph over me.
No one whose hope is in you
    will ever be put to shame,
but they will be put to shame
    who are treacherous without excuse.
Show me your ways, O Lord,
    teach me your paths.

Psalm 25:1–4

$\mathcal{I}$ trust in you, O LORD;
   I say, "You are my God."
My times are in your hands.

Psalm 31:14–15

$\mathcal{W}$e wait in hope for the LORD;
   he is our help and our shield.
In him our hearts rejoice,
   for we trust in his holy name.
May your unfailing love rest upon us, O LORD,
   even as we put our hope in you.

Psalm 33:20–22

Trust in the LORD and do good;
    dwell in the land and enjoy safe pasture.
Delight yourself in the LORD
    and he will give you the desires of your heart.
Commit your way to the LORD;
    trust in him and he will do this:
He will make your righteousness shine like the dawn,
    the justice of your cause like the noonday sun.
Be still before the LORD and wait patiently for him.

Psalm 37:3–7

The Lord is my shepherd, I shall not be in want.
   He makes me lie down in green pastures,
he leads me beside quiet waters,
   he restores my soul.
He guides me in paths of righteousness
   for his name's sake.
Even though I walk
   through the valley of the shadow of death,
I will fear no evil, for you are with me;
your rod and your staff, they comfort me.
You prepare a table before me
   in the presence of my enemies.
You anoint my head with oil; my cup overflows.
Surely goodness and love will follow me
   all the days of my life,
and I will dwell in the house of the Lord
   forever.

Psalm 23

He put a new song in my mouth,
    a hymn of praise to our God.
Many will see and fear
    and put their trust in the Lord....
Many, O Lord my God,
    are the wonders you have done.
The things you planned for us
    no one can recount to you;
were I to speak and tell of them,
    they would be too many to declare.

Psalm 40:3, 5

Find rest, O my soul, in God alone;
　　my hope comes from him.
He alone is my rock and my salvation;
　　he is my fortress, I will not be shaken.
My salvation and my honor depend on God;
　　he is my mighty rock, my refuge.
Trust in him at all times, O people;
　　pour out your hearts to him,
　　for God is our refuge.

Psalm 62:5–8

He who dwells in the shelter of the Most High
    will rest in the shadow of the Almighty.
I will say of the LORD, "He is my refuge and my fortress,
    my God, in whom I trust."
Surely he will save you from the fowler's snare
    and from the deadly pestilence.
He will cover you with his feathers,
    and under his wings you will find refuge;
    his faithfulness will be your shield and rampart.

Psalm 91:1–4

*T*hose who trust in the LORD are like Mount Zion,
    which cannot be shaken but endures forever.
As the mountains surround Jerusalem,
    so the LORD surrounds his people
    both now and forevermore.

Psalm 125:1–2

❧

*A*nswer me quickly, O LORD; . . .
Let the morning bring me word of your unfailing love,
    for I have put my trust in you.
Show me the way I should go,
    for to you I lift up my soul. . . .
I hide myself in you.
Teach me to do your will,
    for you are my God;
may your good Spirit
    lead me on level ground.

Psalm 143:7–10

In God we make our boast all day long,
   and we will praise your name forever.

Psalm 44:8

❧

When I am afraid,
   I will trust in you.
In God, whose word I praise,
   in God I trust; I will not be afraid.
   What can mortal man do to me?

Psalm 56:3–4

❧

You who fear him, trust in the LORD.

Psalm 115:11

THE TREASURE
OF WISDOM

The proverbs of Solomon son of David, king of Israel:
    for attaining wisdom and discipline;
        for understanding words of insight;
    for acquiring a disciplined and prudent life,
        doing what is right and just and fair;
    for giving prudence to the simple,
        knowledge and discretion to the young—
    let the wise listen and add to their learning,
        and let the discerning get guidance.

Proverbs 1:1–5

The fear of the LORD is the beginning of
    knowledge.

Proverbs 1:7

❧

If you accept my words
    and store up my commands within you,
turning your ear to wisdom
    and applying your heart to understanding,
and if you call out for insight
    and cry aloud for understanding,
and if you look for it as for silver
    and search for it as for hidden treasure,
then you will understand the fear of the LORD
    and find the knowledge of God.

Proverbs 2:1–5

The LORD gives wisdom,
  and from his mouth come knowledge and
    understanding.
He holds victory in store for the upright,
  he is a shield to those whose walk is blameless,
for he guards the course of the just
  and protects the way of his faithful ones.
Then you will understand what is right and just
  and fair—every good path.
For wisdom will enter your heart,
  and knowledge will be pleasant to your soul.
Discretion will protect you,
  and understanding will guard you.

Proverbs 2:6–11

Wisdom is more profitable than silver
and yields better returns than gold.
She is more precious than rubies;
nothing you desire can compare with her.
Long life is in her right hand;
in her left hand are riches and honor.
Her ways are pleasant ways,
and all her paths are peace.
She is a tree of life to those who embrace her;
those who lay hold of her will be blessed.

Proverbs 3:14–18

$\mathcal{B}$y wisdom the LORD laid the earth's foundations,
  by understanding he set the heavens in place;
by his knowledge the deeps were divided,
  and the clouds let drop the dew.
Preserve sound judgment and discernment,
  do not let them out of your sight;
they will be life for you,
  an ornament to grace your neck.
Then you will go on your way in safety,
  and your foot will not stumble;
when you lie down, you will not be afraid;
  when you lie down, your sleep will be sweet.

Proverbs 3:19–24

$\mathcal{D}$o not forsake wisdom, and she will protect you;
  love her, and she will watch over you.
Wisdom is supreme; therefore get wisdom.
  Though it cost all you have, get understanding.
Esteem her, and she will exalt you;
  embrace her, and she will honor you.
She will set a garland of grace on your head
  and present you with a crown of splendor....
When you walk, your steps will not be hampered;
  when you run, you will not stumble.
Hold on to instruction, do not let it go;
  guard it well, for it is your life.

Proverbs 4:6–9,12–13

Choose my instruction instead of silver,
    knowledge rather than choice gold,
for wisdom is more precious than rubies,
    and nothing you desire can compare with her.
I, wisdom, dwell together with prudence;
    I possess knowledge and discretion.
To fear the LORD is to hate evil;
    I hate pride and arrogance,
    evil behavior and perverse speech.
Counsel and sound judgment are mine;
    I have understanding and power.
By me kings reign
    and rulers make laws that are just;
by me princes govern,
    and all nobles who rule on earth.
I love those who love me,
    and those who seek me find me.

Proverbs 8:10–17

With me [wisdom] are riches and honor,
  enduring wealth and prosperity.
My fruit is better than fine gold;
  what I yield surpasses choice silver.
I walk in the way of righteousness,
  along the paths of justice,
bestowing wealth on those who love me
  and making their treasuries full.
The LORD brought me forth as the first of his works,
  before his deeds of old;
I was appointed from eternity,
  from the beginning, before the world began.
When there were no oceans, I was given birth,
  when there were no springs abounding with water;
before the mountains were settled in place,
  before the hills, I was given birth,
before he made the earth or its fields
  or any of the dust of the world.

Proverbs 8:18–26

Say to wisdom, "You are my sister,"
    and call understanding your kinsman.

Proverbs 7:4

❧

Wisdom calls out, "I was there when the LORD set the
        heavens in place,
    when he marked out the horizon on the face of the
        deep,
when he established the clouds above
    and fixed securely the fountains of the deep,
when he gave the sea its boundary
    so the waters would not overstep his command,
and when he marked out the foundations of the earth.
    Then I was the craftsman at his side.
I was filled with delight day after day,
    rejoicing always in his presence,
rejoicing in his whole world
    and delighting in mankind."

Proverbs 8:27–31

When pride comes, then comes disgrace,
  but with humility comes wisdom.
The integrity of the upright guides them,
  but the unfaithful are destroyed by their duplicity.

Proverbs 11:2–3

❧

Wisdom is found in those who take advice.

Proverbs 13:10

❧

The wisdom of the prudent is to give thought to
  their ways.

Proverbs 14:8

❧

How much better to get wisdom than gold,
  to choose understanding rather than silver!

Proverbs 16:16

*A*pply your heart to instruction
   and your ears to words of knowledge....
Listen to your father, who gave you life,
   and do not despise your mother when she is old.
Buy the truth and do not sell it;
   get wisdom, discipline and understanding.

Proverbs 23:12, 22–23

❧

*B*y wisdom a house is built,
   and through understanding it is established;
through knowledge its rooms are filled
   with rare and beautiful treasures.

Proverbs 24:3–4

❧

*K*now also that wisdom is sweet to your soul;
   if you find it, there is a future hope for you,
   and your hope will not be cut off.

Proverbs 24:14

A wife of noble character who can find?
  She is worth far more than rubies....
She is clothed with strength and dignity;
  she can laugh at the days to come.
She speaks with wisdom,
  and faithful instruction is on her tongue.
She watches over the affairs of her household
  and does not eat the bread of idleness.
Her children arise and call her blessed;
  her husband also, and he praises her:
"Many women do noble things, but you surpass
    them all."

Proverbs 31:10, 25–29

$\mathscr{S}$urely you desire truth in the inner parts;
 you teach me wisdom in the inmost place.
Cleanse me with hyssop, and I will be clean;
 wash me, and I will be whiter than snow.
Let me hear joy and gladness; . . .
Hide your face from my sins
 and blot out all my iniquity.
Create in me a pure heart, O God,
 and renew a steadfast spirit within me.
Do not cast me from your presence
 or take your Holy Spirit from me.
Restore to me the joy of your salvation
 and grant me a willing spirit, to sustain me.
Then I will teach transgressors your ways,
 and sinners will turn back to you.

Psalm 51:6–13

Teach us to number our days aright,
   that we may gain a heart of wisdom....
   Have compassion on your servants.
Satisfy us in the morning with your unfailing love,
   that we may sing for joy and be glad all our days.
May your deeds be shown to your servants,
   your splendor to their children.
May the favor of the Lord our God rest upon us;
   establish the work of our hands for us.

Psalm 90:12–14, 16–17

How many are your works, O LORD!
   In wisdom you made them all;
   the earth is full of your creatures.

Psalm 104:24

❧

The fear of the LORD is the beginning of wisdom;
   all who follow his precepts have good
      understanding.
To him belongs eternal praise.

Psalm 111:10

❧

Every word of God is flawless;
   he is a shield to those who take refuge in him.

Proverbs 30:5

THE LOVE OF GOD, FAMILY AND FRIENDS

A friend loves at all times,
   and a brother is born for adversity.

Proverbs 17:17

❧

*T*here is a friend who sticks closer than a brother.

Proverbs 18:24

❧

*B*etter is open rebuke
   than hidden love.
Wounds from a friend can be trusted, . . .
Perfume and incense bring joy to the heart,
   and the pleasantness of one's friend springs from his
   earnest counsel.

Proverbs 27:5–6, 9

$\mathcal{D}$o not forsake your friend and the friend of your
   father, . . .
   better a neighbor nearby than a brother far away.

Proverbs 27:10

❧

$\mathcal{W}$ho walks with the wise grows wise.

Proverbs 13:20

❧

$\mathcal{I}$ will praise you, O Lord, among the nations;
   I will sing of you among the peoples.
For great is your love, reaching to the heavens;
   your faithfulness reaches to the skies.
Be exalted, O God, above the heavens;
   let your glory be over all the earth.

Psalm 57:9–11

*Y*our love is ever before me,
I love the house where you live, O LORD,
    the place where your glory dwells.
My feet stand on level ground;
    in the great assembly I will praise the LORD.

Psalm 26:3, 8, 12

❧

*H*ow great is your goodness,
    which you have stored up for those who fear you,
which you bestow … on those who take refuge in you.…
Love the LORD, all his saints!
    The LORD preserves the faithful.

Psalm 31:19, 23

$\mathcal{R}$ejoice in the LORD and be glad, you righteous;
sing, all you who are upright in heart!

Psalm 32:11

❧

$\mathcal{S}$ing joyfully to the LORD, you righteous;
it is fitting for the upright to praise him.

Psalm 33:1

❧

$\mathcal{T}$he eyes of the LORD are on those who fear him,
on those whose hope is in his unfailing love.

Psalm 33:18

❧

$\mathcal{T}$he angel of the LORD encamps around
those who fear him,
and he delivers them.

Psalm 34:7

$\mathcal{O}$ LORD, by your hand save me...
You still the hunger of those you cherish;
  their sons have plenty,
and they store up wealth for their children.
And I—in righteousness will see your face;
  when I awake, I will be satisfied with seeing your
    likeness.

Psalm 17:14–15

❧

$\mathcal{G}$ive thanks to the LORD, for he is good;
  his love endures forever.

Psalm 106:1

I do not hide your righteousness in my heart;
    I speak of your faithfulness and salvation.
I do not conceal your love and your truth
    from the great assembly....
May all who seek you
    rejoice and be glad in you;
may those who love your salvation always say,
    "The Lord be exalted!"

Psalm 40:10, 16

❧

Let heaven and earth praise him,
    the seas and all that move in them,
for God will save Zion
    and rebuild the cities of Judah.
Then people will settle there and possess it;
    the children of his servants will inherit it,
    and those who love his name will dwell there.

Psalm 69:34–36

Let love and faithfulness never leave you;
  bind them around your neck,
  write them on the tablet of your heart.
Then you will win favor and a good name
  in the sight of God and man.

Proverbs 3:3–4

❧

Know that the LORD is God.
  It is he who made us, and we are his;
  we are his people, the sheep of his pasture.
Enter his gates with thanksgiving
  and his courts with praise;
  give thanks to him and praise his name.
For the LORD is good and his love endures forever;
  his faithfulness continues through all generations.

Psalm 100:3–5